BODIE

Boom Town—Gold Town

The Last of California's
Old-time Mining Camps

by Douglas McDonald

Published in Cooperation with The Friends of Bodie

NEVADA PUBLICATIONS
Box 15444
Las Vegas, Nevada 89114

THE
FRIENDS OF
BODIE

WHEN YOU VISIT

Bodie State Historic Park is best visited during the summer. At other times the weather is unpredictable. Off-season visitors are cautioned to check at the Mono County Sheriff's office in Bridgeport for road and weather conditions before making the trip. Roads are often difficult; trailers are not advised. Over-snow equipment (snowmobiles, skis, snow shoes, etc.) may be required to reach the park during the winter months.

The Park is open year-round; 9:00 a.m. to 7:00 p.m. in the summer months, and 9:00 a.m. to 4:00 p.m. the rest of the year. An entrance fee is charged year-round.

For more information about Bodie SHP you may contact the park either by writing to:

BODIE STATE HISTORIC PARK
Post Office Box 515
Bridgeport, California 93517

or by calling the park directly at:
(619) 647-6445

PLEASE HELP US

- DON'T TOUCH ANYTHING: leave every rock and rusty can in place for our grandchildren to see.
- WATCH OUT: this is a real ghost town; splinters, nails and broken glass are everywhere.
- DON'T SMOKE: except in the parking lot.
- The Mill Area is hazardous; please stay out.
- Unless otherwise noted, all buildings are closed to the public.

DEPARTMENT OF PARKS & RECREATION
State of California – The Resources Agency
P.O. Box 942896 Sacramento, CA 94296-0838

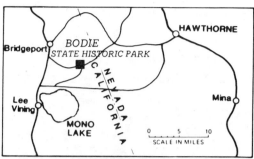

VICINITY MAP

The Friends of Bodie is a group dedicated to the preservation of the gold mining ghost town of Bodie. It is a chapter of the Tahoe-Sierra State Parks Association. This is a volunteer, non-profit organization which helps preserve and interpret state parks in the Sierra District of the State Department of Parks and Recreation.

In 1962 Bodie became a state historic park. This did not automatically insure all structures and artifacts would be properly preserved. Within the State Park System Bodie must compete with other parks for funding and priority projects. Likewise, the Department of Parks and Recreation must compete with all other state agencies for limited amounts of funding.

The Friends of Bodie can help raise funds and provide volunteer support to insure that Bodie is properly preserved.

Financial support and volunteer workers are vital in preserving Bodie. Should you wish to participate in this effort please contact:

The Friends of Bodie
Post Office Box 515
Bridgeport, CA 93517

Picture Credits are as follows:

Bodie State Park, 38 bottom, 39 bottom, back cover.
(courtesy of Brad Sturdivant)

J. Ross Browne sketches, 5, 6 top, 8 top.

Fred Holabird, 19 bottom.

Helen "Dude" McInnis, Front Cover, 22 bottom, 34,
35, 37 bottom, 38 top, 39 top, 43 bottom, 46.

Author's Collection, 21 top, 27 bottom.

Publisher's Collection, 6 bottom, 8 bottom, 9, 10,
16 top, 27 top, 36 top.

All other pictures, amounting to about half of the
book, are from the Emil Billeb Collection,
(courtesy of Vickie Daniels).

ISBN 0-913814-88-1

PRINTED IN THE UNITED STATES OF AMERICA

BODIE—
BOOM TOWN — GOLD TOWN
The Last of California's
Old-time Mining Camps

At the height of the boom in 1879-1880, Bodie was so rough and wicked that shootings, stabbings, and thefts took place nearly every day. But the local badmen who gave the town such a violent reputation did not bother the gold-crazed crowd, because the mines were the center of attention throughout the West.

Perhaps to make Bodie a synonym for violence and toughness, a rival mining camp newspaper quoted a young girl in 1879, on learning that her family was moving to the camp, as reportedly saying, "Goodbye, God! We're going to Bodie!"

Such an insult did not go unnoticed. The belligerent *Bodie Daily Free Press* quickly corrected this, claiming that there had been a typographical error in the printed story. What she really said, according to the newspaper, was "Good! By God! We're going to Bodie!"

Wells Drury, the famous editor of Virginia City, Nevada, remembered a remark made by a local undertaker which enhanced Bodie's notorious violence. The mortician said, "We never get any breaks in this business here in Virginia City. As soon as the local talent gets to thinking they're tough they go try it out in Bodie and Bodie undertakers get the job of burying them."

In the Beginning...

Town of Mono

Gold was first discovered in this area in 1857 at Dogtown, twelve miles west of present-day Bodie. By the time this small boom died two years later, another gold region was developing at Monoville, a few miles farther south. These original locations prompted prospectors to venture further afield in search of additional mining sites.

Late in 1859 a German from New York, William (or Waterman) S. Bodey uncovered a vein of gold at the foot of Bodie Bluff, supposedly while shoveling to retrieve a wounded rabbit which had taken refuge in a hole. Enough prospectors and miners came to these wind-swept hills that within a year a mining district was organized, named for the original discoverer who unfortunately perished in a blizzard shortly after making his find. By 1862 the district's name had evolved into Bodie because of a careless misspelling on a sign, according to local legend.

In the early 1860's the fledgling Bodie mines began to be worked, but they were always overshadowed by the spectacular development of the gold mines in nearby Esmeralda Mining District centered at Aurora, just 12 miles to the northeast in Nevada. The camp of Bodie gained only passing attention, and by 1864 one observer counted no more than 20 wood-frame buildings.

Desultory mining continued over the next few years, although a social life developed as some families joined the camp's single miners. Bodie's first wedding took place in December 1867 when Rodger Horner married Marietta Butler. They bore a son in April 1869, the first birth at Bodie.

Sketch by
J. Ross Browne,
Bodie, 1864

Bodie Bluff at left.

AURORA: SILVER SUITE

The gold camp of Bodie's rich Nevada neighbor, Aurora, was a flourishing silver mining boom camp in the early 1860's. Its wealth was amply demonstrated by the presence of several substantial two-story brick buildings on the main street, while Bodie only had a few wood-frame buildings. Beyond the town, the canyon in the background leads to Bodie, 12 miles distant by stagecoach. While Aurora's surface bonanzas were exhausted by 1869, after yielding more than $29 million, Bodie would boom after the mid-1870's, producing at least $30 million.

BODIE BLUFF.

J. Ross Browne sketched Bodie Bluff, the district's most prominent landmark, when he visited the new camp in 1864. The Bodie Bluff Consolidated Mining Company, with a capitalization of $1.1 million, failed only months after original incorporation in 1863. It was Joseph Wasson and other promoters who really put Bodie on the map through extensive publicity in California, issuing maps of the Bodie townsite which showed the principal claims.

INCORPORATED JANUARY 26, 1863.

Capital Stock, $1,110,000.

Bodie Bluff Consolidation Mining C

No.

This Certifies, That

is the owner of

in the Capital Stock of the **Bodie Bluff Consolidation Mining Compa**

Transferable on the Books of the Company, by endorsement hereon, and surrender of this Certificate.

Aurora, Mono Go., C

11,100 Shares, $100 Each.

Agnew & Deffebach print, S. F.

Secretary.

Presid

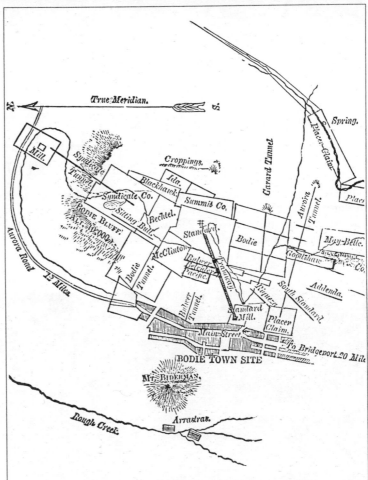

The main rush to Bodie began with the formation of the Standard Mining Co. in April 1877. Originally located in 1861 as the Bunker Hill Mine, this property became part of the first mining company incorporated in this district in 1863. Known as the Bodie Bluff Consolidated, and owned in part by Leland Stanford and Judge F. T. Bechtel, this venture failed in less than a year.

Believed to be worthless by 1873, the Bunker Hill property changed hands several times until an unexpected cave-in revealed a fabulously rich ore chamber. In late 1877, spearheaded by the rich ore shipments form the Standard Co. mines, a real mining stampede to Bodie got underway.

As Virginia City's mines began to decline about that same time, many former Comstockers swelled the local population into the thousands. In July 1879 the *Bodie Daily News* claimed a population of 8,000 people for the camp, including transients, at the height of the boom. One newspaper account stated, "The growth of the town has no parallel in the history of mining...Society has not assimilated, but the elements exist in a state of chaos. Fine residences, saloons, business

A BIRDSEYE VIEW OF THE MINING DISTRICT AND THE TOWN OF BODIE, MONO COUNTY, CALIFORNIA

The sketch below was specially drawn for *Daily Stock Report* in 1879. It shows the principal features of the Bodie mining district, looking east, dramatically portraying the large bluffs and ore-bearing hills of the district. Below them is the Bodie town site and the Standard Mill, whose tramway directly connected to the mineral-rich lodes. Other hoisting works and mills are shown amid roadways and tunneling.

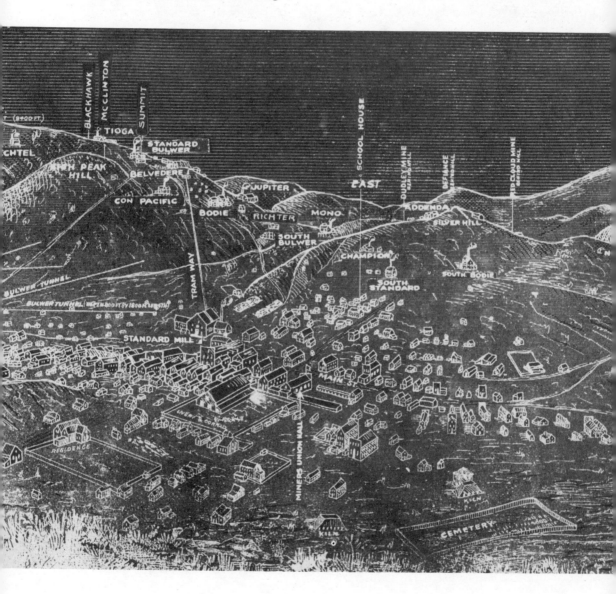

houses, brothels and cabins are in a motley jumble as to location. There are 47 saloons and 10 faro tables. This is not a disparagement of the district, but an evidence of its prosperity....There are however two banking houses, five wholesale stores, and an excellent daily newspaper, and all the accessories of civilization and refinement will soon follow."

Bodie's reputation as a tough town was emphasized by newspapers where such sensationalism was found to increase sales. Throughout the spring of 1878 accounts of shootings and sundry violence in the booming mining camp were avidly reported throughout the country which prompted E.H. Clough to pen a fictional parody of these events. Originally published early in the June 1 issue of *The Argonaut,* it was soon reprinted all across the nation. This is credited as the origin of the term "Bad Man of Bodie" which soon became the "Bad Man *From* Bodie," a generic term for the large number of "roughs" in the community.

Though myth soon outdistanced the truth, Bodie was indeed plagued with more than its share of mayhem. Not infrequently there was a "man for breakfast" because of early morning gunplay. A visiting journalist wrote of the virtual shooting gallery at Bodie, noting that "six shooters were of no account unless used."

"Within a fortnight," complained one reporter in 1880, "town men have been seriously beaten over the head with six shooters, one has been shot, one stabbed to death, one man and one woman have been knifed, one woman's skull crushed with a club, and she may die tonight. For these seven crimes—for these five lives jeopardized and two taken—two arrests have been made."

"I recall one spectacular fight between a fine young miner, who had gone somewhat wild, and a 'sure-thing gambler'" wrote Grant Smith, an attorney who arrived in 1879. "They had quarreled and then partly made it up when the gambler invited the miner to take a drink. As they stood side by side at the bar, the gambler drew a gun and shot the miner in the back. The miner drew his gun, and they stood holding each other by the coat and shooting until they fell to the floor. The miner died instantly; the gambler lived for some years, a physical wreck."

Bodie's citizens finally took matters into their own hands late in January 1881. Johnny Treloar, a well-liked Cornish miner, quarreled with a Frenchman named Joseph DeRoche, who insisted on dancing with Treloar's wife at the Miner's Union Hall. When the two men stepped outside into the street, DeRoche calmly pulled a pistol and shot Treloar in the head, killing him instantly.

To Agents Wells, Fargo & Co.—Don't Post, but place these Circulars in the hands of Officers and discreet persons only.

ARREST
Stage Robber and Murderer!

About two o'clock in the morning of May 13th, 1879, an attempt was made by one man to stop and rob the ingoing stage three miles before reaching Aurora, Esmeralda County, Nevada.

At daylight Officer Harrington, with three Indians, took the track, and when about eight miles out was fired on several times by the robber, the second shot killing one of the Indians. Pursuit was then given up, but afterward he was traced into and through Mono County, California, and into Tuolumne County as far as Sonora, since which time nothing has been heard from him. Was in Sonora Monday Night, May 19th.

DESCRIPTION.

L. E. or P. L. SHORT, worked from the middle of March until May 1st herding sheep for a Mr. Kilgore, who keeps the Mountain House, on the Carson and Aurora Stage Road, first station north from Wellington's. Came from Winnemucca to Kilgore's; claims to be from Fort Scott, Kansas; an American, about 26 years old; full 6 feet tall; very erect and bony; pretty broad shoulders; full beard and moustache, but not very heavy, and inclined to sandy; long brown hair, straight and cut square around the neck; steps very long when walking; drinks and smokes; wore black sack coat with two buttons behind; black hat very slouchy; brown pants; boots with nails in soles; rather green and gawky looking; sold his breech loading carbine, with which he did the killing, at first station west of Summit.

The State of Nevada has a Standing Reward of $250, and Wells, Fargo & Co. $300 for the arrest and conviction of such offenders.

Should he be arrested, telegraph the undersigned at Sacramento, who will take him to Aurora without expense to party arresting.

Note carefully everything he says of his movements during the month of May. Preserve his boots, and every article of clothing, etc., he may have.

J. B. HUME,
Special Officer W. F. & Co.

Sacramento, June 3d, 1879.

Although DeRoche was quickly arrested, others in Bodie fumed over the case. When the killer managed to escape from the constable guarding him, a local vigilante group quickly formed a posse which soon apprehended the prisoner and returned him to the jail. Shortly after 1 a.m. on January 17, about 200 men quietly advanced upon the jail and removed the prisoner. He was quickly escorted to Webber's blacksmith shop, where the mob borrowed a huge gallows frame used for repairing wagons. This was set up at the corner of Main and Lowe Streets, the site of Treloar's murder, and within minutes DeRoche was hanged from it. This was the only instance where Bodie's "601" conducted a lynching, although several times just a warning from this group sent truly undesirable characters packing.

A clever newspaperman turned usual incidents into a humorous story. The *Bodie Evening Miner* on March 18, 1884 reported, "At five o'clock this morning Billy Deegan and Felix Donnelly had a duel on Main Street, at long range. Nine shots were exchanged, but nobody was hurt, not even a bystander was killed—and at that early hour there were many standing around ready to catch any stray ball that came their way...There is not a case of sickness in Bodie and were it not for the numerous shooting affrays that keep up a supply of wounded, our physicians could take a rest."

One of the most unusual shooting affrays occurred in August 1879, when two rival mining companies quarreled over ownership of ground containing a new shaft. One group barricaded itself in the mine workings while the other attacked with guns blazing. Only one man was killed in the unsuccessful attack, but the local miners' union was in an uproar. In an unprecedented move, hundreds of union men marched to the barricaded mine, driving away the defenders.

Not long after, the union succeeded in forcing George Daly, the mine manager who had successfully defended the shaft from attack, out of town. Many people spoke out vehemently against the powers the union had usurped, but Daly went on to a successful mining career in Colorado.

Bodie Settles Down

The town's powerful miners' union, the first such union organized in California, was founded on January 15, 1878. Originally created to improve working conditions and maintain uniform wages, the union soon constructed a large hall which became the center of social activities, dances, lectures and various meetings.

Bodie always had a strong business community, which originally developed to serve the crowds who flocked to town from outlying camps. In particular, Bodie's newspapers were a source of much liveliness. The *Standard* began publication in October 1877, followed by the *Morning News* in March 1879, the *Daily Free Press* in September 1879, and the *Bodie Evening Miner* in May 1882. These newspapers maintained a lively rivalry, especially with papers in other towns. When the *Carson Daily Free Press* commented that "the weather is so cold in Bodie that four pairs of blankets and three in a bed is not sufficient to promote warmth," the *Daily Free Press* took offense. "You are a brainless liar," responded the Bodie paper. "The weather here... is too warm during the day for convenience as stiffs can not be kept any length of time without being packed in ice."

Another editor once praised a Bodie paper by commenting, "For a one horse paper, starting on a one horse basis, and doing business in a one horse way, by a one horse man, the progress of the *Bodie Evening Miner* has been wonderfully upward and onward." There was never a lack of news in Bodie during its heyday, and it is because of these competitive and entertaining newspapers that many lively tales have been preserved.

Other businesses prospered during the boom. The firm of Gilson & Barber opened a huge general merchandise store in November 1877, reported to be the largest of its kind in the Intermountain West. So many goods were sold during this winter that the company's freight bill alone was nearly $100,000.

By mid-1879, the commercial streets contained more than 50 saloons, numerous gambling halls, six restaurants, seven barber shops, four lodging houses, two livery stables, three breweries, a post office, the ever-present Wells Fargo office, and countless small shops continuing grocers, fruit vendors, booteries, butchers, tinsmiths, jewelers, saddle makers, drug stores, bakeries, doctors and attorneys. The red light district housed numerous brothels, and included such residents as the now-famous Rosa May.

Bodie also had a Chinese population, which numbered about 350 by 1880. Besides cutting cordwood and selling it to the community,

Many of the Chinese who lived in Bodie worked as woodcutters, often transporting their product by burro train. although more than 18,000 cords of wood were stockpiled in town by late 1879, the demand had grown so great by April 1880 that firewood brought $25 per cord. In October 1878, one shipment of wood from Carson City to Bodie contained 50,000 board feet of clear lumber, all hauled into town on freight wagons (below). In another instance, 40 lumber teams were on the Big Meadows & Bodie Toll Road at the same time. It was this enormous demand for wood and lumber which prompted the construction of the Bodie Railway & Lumber Co.'s line to Mono Mills, 35 miles south of Bodie, in a forested area.

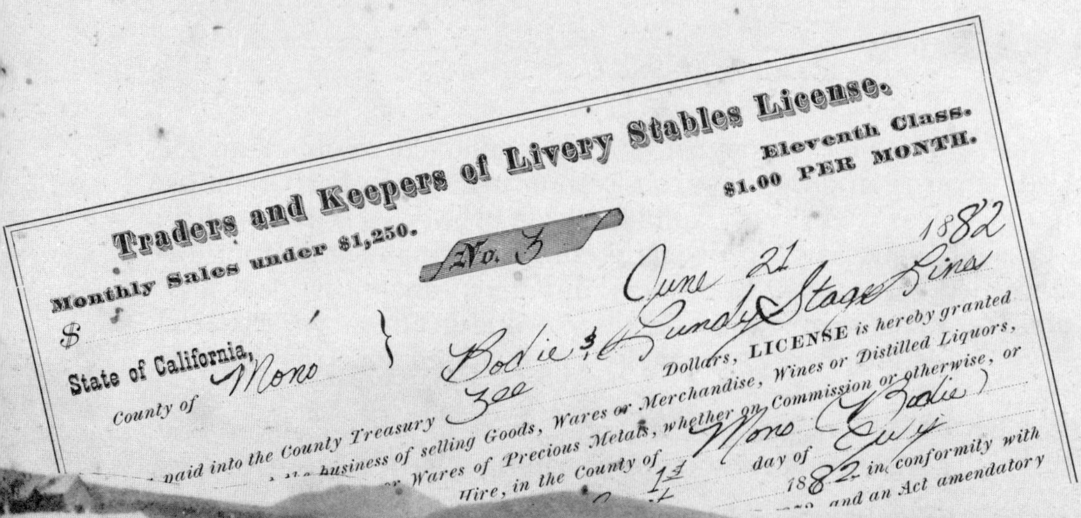

Traders and Keepers of Livery Stables License.
Eleventh Class.
$1.00 PER MONTH.

Monthly Sales under $1,250.

No. 3

$ ....

State of California,
County of *Mono* }

June 21 1882

Bodie & Lundy Stage Line

.... Dollars, LICENSE is hereby granted

.... paid into the County Treasury .... the business of selling Goods, Wares or Merchandise, Wines or Distilled Liquors, ... or Wares of Precious Metals, whether on Commission or otherwise, or .... Hire, in the County of *Mono* .... *1st* day of .... 188*2* in conformity with .... and an Act amendatory

Mono Bodie

LUMBER YARD IN BODIE
BEFORE THE ADVENT
OF THE RAILROAD

Bodie required hundreds of tons of wood per year. Heavy timbers
supported mine workings, thousands of board feet went into
constructing new buildings, cordwood was constantly consumed
by the mines' and mills' boilers, and every building needed plenty
of firewood for heating during the long, severe winters.

The completion of the Bodie Railway & Lumber Company in 1881 enabled greater amounts of wood and lumber to be brought into the camp. Trees cut south of Mono Lake were hauled by mule teams to Mono Mills, sawn to their needed dimensions, and transported by rail to Bodie.

Excursions on the Bodie Railway, renamed the Mono Lake Railway in 1906, were never an official practice as this line never carried passengers. However, one enterprising individual used an automobile adapted to run on rails to transport men and equipment.

Orientals also operated laundries and opium dens. Throughout the boom years many efforts were made to close down the dens, especially as they catered to everyone, including white women and minor children. But as the general population declined in the mid-1880's, the Chinese moved on to other locales.

Local banks did well during the peak years but ran into trouble when the boom began to fade. The Mono County Bank of Bodie was incorporated in August 1877, and the Bank of Bodie (Bodie Bank) opened its doors 12 months later. The Bodie Bank suspended in 1882, followed by the failure of the Mono County Bank in 1886. The Bodie Bank did manage to reopen under new management and struggle through the town's declining years only to be destroyed by fire in 1932.

Bodie's population consisted mainly of single men, which gave rise to a large number of hotels and austere rooming houses. The earliest was the boarding house of the Empire Mill & Mining Co., which opened for business in the early 1860's. For several years it was run by William O'Hara, one of the West's few well-respected negro businessmen, who was also the manager of the mining company.

The town did boast one first-class hotel—The Grand Central. The ground floor had a handsome barroom, a reading room, an elegant 16 by 44-foot dining room, and a large hall. On the second floor were 21 well-furnished rooms and private parlor overlooking the main street.

Exorbitant prices were paid for rough-sawn lumber, especially at the peak of the boom when one writer reported 30 new buildings under construction at the same time. Even more important was the need for cordwood to power boilers in the mines and mills and for warming everyone through the harsh winters. When the camp ran out of wood early in 1880, discussions arose over the proposed construction of a railroad to supply Bodie with this necessary commodity.

The Bodie Railway and Lumber Co. was organized in February 1881, and the last spike was driven that November. When completed, the narrow gauge railroad hauled timber from Mono Mills, seven miles south of Mono Lake, a distance of 31-1/2 miles to Bodie. No passengers ever rode on this line, which never connected to an outside railroad system. Its name was changed to the Bodie & Benton RR in 1882, then it took back its original name in 1893. Once more renamed in 1906, this time to the Mono Lake Railway and Lumber Co., the little line stayed in operation until its abandonment in 1917.

Life was seldom dull in remote Bodie. Residents created their own entertainment, particularly the respectable women of the town. "It would be difficult to find a finer type than those old-time mining camp women," recalled Grant Smith. "It was remarkable how much they did in the way of getting up theatrical performances, dances, suppers, Sunday picnics, sleighing parties, and other diversions."

Like the adults in town, Bodie's children often created their own entertainment. "Amusements were few and simple, and all the more enjoyed," wrote Grant Smith, who arrived in Bodie in 1879 when 14 years old.

The Bank of Bodie, organized with just $30,000 in capital, began issuing these ornate checks shortly after opening in a sturdy building on Main Street in the fall of 1878. Although it suspended in 1886 due to Bodie's decline, the bank reopened and was purchased in 1890 by J.S. Cain, shown here standing in front of his vault. Cain continued to operate this bank until it was leveled by fire in 1932.

A public school opened on March 5, 1878 with Belle Moore instructing 10 students. The first small schoolhouse was burned down by a tough kid who didn't want to attend. So many children moved to town that the two-story Bon Ton Lodging House was converted to Bodie's schoolhouse in January 1879.

The boom years saw a marked increase in the number of school-age children in town, who filled the town's schoolhouse. At first the tougher children ran roughshod over schoolmaster Cook, but eventually the school settled down when a new schoolmaster named McCarty began to use an iron stove poker to enforce discipline. Even after the boom peaked and the population began to dwindle, Bodie's families kept the classes filled for several decades.

Although the Reverend Hinkle began holding services in the Miners' Union Hall in 1878, it was not until September 15, 1882 that the Methodist Church was completed. Bodie's only other church building, the Roman Catholic "St. John the Baptist," was also completed in 1882, though it burned in a mysterious fire in 1928. The interior of the Methodist Church featured a large plaque behind the altar, upon which were written the Ten Commandments.

By 1928, Bodie's main street, lined with a few dozen empty wooden buildings, had taken on the appearance of a true ghost town.

ain street - Bodie, Calif.

"Bodie is a lively little place," commented the *Standard* about the weekend before Christmas, 1878. "We have no church, but Miners' Union Hall answers that and a variety of other purposes. On Saturday evening, for instance, the hall was occupied for a 'grand testimonial and complimentary benefit to Billy Costello, the champion lightweight of the Pacific Coast, matched to fight Harry Maynard for $1,000 a side.' This performance closed with a rattling 'passage at arms' between Billy Costello and Cassidy.

At 10 o'clock Sunday morning the Rev. Father Cassin of the Roman Catholic Church, said mass in the same place, but dismissed his congregation in time to allow the Rev. G. B. Hinckle, of the Methodist Episcopal Church, to preach to his little flock at 2 p.m. In the evening the platform of the same hall was occupied by an amateur minstrel performance...All of which goes to show great catholicity on the part of the Union as to the use of their hall, and a generous and harmonious use of it by a singular variety of interests."

Although Methodist and Roman Catholic services continued to be held in the Miners' Union Hall from 1878 on, there was insufficient support among the 6,000 residents to build a church. Finally in 1882, after the boom had peaked, both denominations dedicated houses of worship.

Everyone participated in celebrating major holidays, especially the 4th of July. The town was decorated with young trees which were cut in the mountains and brought into town, and placed in buckets along both sides of Main Street. The highlight of the day's events was a huge parade which attracted participants from the various fraternal organizations, several military groups, baseball clubs, wagons filled with young girls, local citizens, and a contingent of Mexican Patriots.

Even in the depth of winter, when deep snow drifts blanketed Bodie, Christmas celebrations involved the whole town. Two large trees were set up in the Miners' Union Hall, and nearly every family in town brought gifts to place under them. The trees were lit with candles while men stood by with wet sponges on long poles to guard against fire. Plenty of food and drink was provided, with the long-awaited party lasting through the night.

Promoter Joseph Wasson issued this mining report of Bodie and nearby Aurora in the spring of 1878 to induce moneyed San Franciscans to invest in the mines and mills east of the Sierra, particularly Bodie and Aurora. This 60-page booklet gives detailed descriptions of the Bodie mines, travel routes, and the promise of railroad service. As evidence of ownership in the mines, the company issued handsomely engraved stock certificates signed by corporate officers.

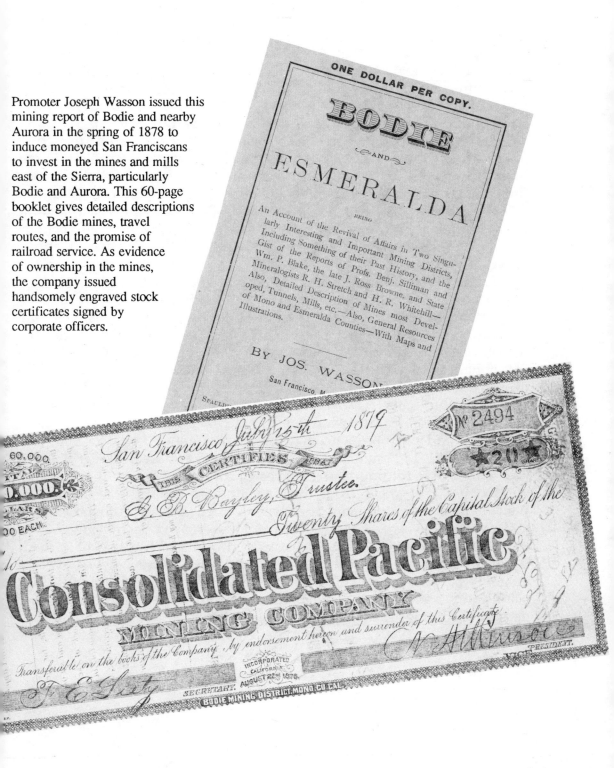

The Long Decline

Bodie's boom began to fade in 1881 and by November the population dipped below 3,000. In April, 1882 J. Kallman wrote to his banker in Carson City that "I think we will have a lively boom in Bodie stock this summer," but he was mistaken. Several of the major mines closed down that year and by 1887 only 1,500 people remained in town. Vacant buildings began to be hauled away to other mining camps.

During its heyday Bodie had fortunately been spared disastrous fires such as those which nearly wiped out contemporary mining towns like Virginia City, Pioche, and Hamilton, Nevada. The first small fire to break out in February 1878 led to the organization of a volunteer fire department. By 1880 Bodie had four fire companies keeping the town safe through many attempts at arson and several small accidental blazes. However, the fire companies gradually disbanded as the population declined.

Bodie's remaining fire-fighting equipment was unable to handle a restaurant fire which broke out in July 1892. Someone had turned off the water to the hydrants along Main Street. By the time this was remedied, and various pieces of equipment had been brought up, the fire blazed out of control. When it was finally extinguished, much of Main Street had been leveled. Vacant buildings on side streets were relocated to fill empty lots, but several major structures were forever lost.

Later that same year, Bodie became the site of the nation's first electrical power transmission for industrial purposes. Prior to 1892, electricity had only been used where it was generated. The Standard Co. built a 12-1/2 mile power line from Green Creek straight to its mill, carefully avoiding sharp curves or angles as it was thought that electricity might shoot from the line at these points. The success of this venture revolutionized the use of electricity in industry, but it took another 18 years before the town of Bodie enjoyed electric power.

In 1899 the wood-frame Standard Mill burned but it was immediately rebuilt with the addition of a cyanide plant, a newly developed gold recovery process. The new complex of corrugated tin buildings stands on the site today. Bodie's mines continued to operate for another decade, bringing the district's total production to more than $30 million, but after 1910 the smaller mines began to close permanently.

This battery of five stamps was installed in the second Standard mill, constructed after the first mill burned in 1899. These heavy iron stamps were used to pulverize gold- and silver-bearing ore as it entered the mill for reduction.

The mining and milling process ends when a millhand pours the liquid ore, now separated from the waste rock, into a bullion bar, in the melting room. The millhand keeps a safe distance from the hot buckets by use of a block and tackle. In nearly 90 years of production the Bodie district produced a recorded $21 million in gold and silver, most of it leaving the camp in ingots such as those stacked (below), ready for shipment from the Standard plant.

Bodie's boom peaked in 1880, and over the next several years mine production and the population dwindled away. The Standard Company began successfully utilizing the then-new cyanide reduction process in 1899, but the resurgence of mining activity which this produced lasted only until 1909.

Unlike most western mining towns, Bodie saw few fires during the boom years. However, later fires, such as the burning of the Standard Mill in 1898, hastened the town's demise. This mill was rebuilt, and local mining experienced a brief resurgence, but by 1909 Bodie was again in decline. The burning of the mill's cyanide plant (below) occurred in 1947.

The San Francisco *Chronicle* reported in 1921 that only 30 people remained and many of the buildings were being demolished by local ranchers for their lumber. Yet the town retained sufficient spunk that a small tourist economy began to develop in the 1930's at the same time that new technology produced a minor revival in mining.

Bodie's fledgling tourist trade suffered a setback in 1930 when prohibition agents raided 14 businesses and forced the proprietors to each post a $1,500 bond. This drastic move even led famous humorist Will Rogers to comment on the town's attempt to stage a comeback being seriously hampered by the "destruction of all liquid refreshment."

Then on June 23, 1932 Bodie was once more ravaged by fire. Started by a boy playing with matches, the flames spread quickly through the dry wood-frame buildings. By day's end most business buildings had gone up in smoke, including the Occidental Hotel, Butterfly Saloon, U.S. Hotel, Bodie Bank and Masonic Hall.

The town was never rebuilt. Jim Cain, Bodie's principal landholder and the last resident remaining from the days when the "Bad Man From Bodie" was a by-word coast to coast, was nevertheless optimistic, even while standing amid the ruins of his own bank.

"The total production of the Bodie district is estimated at $50 to $60 million," claimed Cain. "We expect a revival; the new price for gold is most interesting and causing many inquiries for gold mines and leases in placers and quartz mines. The mines are equipped, ready to start operations, all electric and modern machinery. Some are operating and shipping bullion."

Actually, only very limited mining continued at Bodie until the Standard Co.'s cyanide plant was forever crippled by a fire in 1947. The venerable old camp's reverses had been due to error, its own and others. In the words of a song popular in years past:

> He had sand in his craw,
> But was slow on the draw;
> So we planted him 'neath the daisies.

That was Bodie, in the color of its youth and vitality. It was gold that produced the heritage, building character in its citizens, and this shall not be forgotten. Through the efforts of the Cain family, the remaining sun-browned wooden structures were protected until the entire townsite became a California State Historic Park in 1962.

Tens of thousands visit Bodie annually for a glimpse into the past of the state's most famous gold mining town. "Bodie was unique," Grant Smith later recalled. "It was the last of the old-time mining camps; the last, in type, of the pioneer days of California."

As late as 1930 Bodie's residents still turned out to celebrate important holidays. One of the most difficult events held on Labor Day was the mucking contest, where miners raced against the clock to shovel broken rock into an ore car.

Independence Day celebrations were always important events in Bodie. Saplings placed in buckets and tied to awning supports lined Main Street, where most of the day's activities took place. In the popular drilling contests, miners attempted to sink their hand drills the farthest distance into a granite boulder in a set number of minutes.

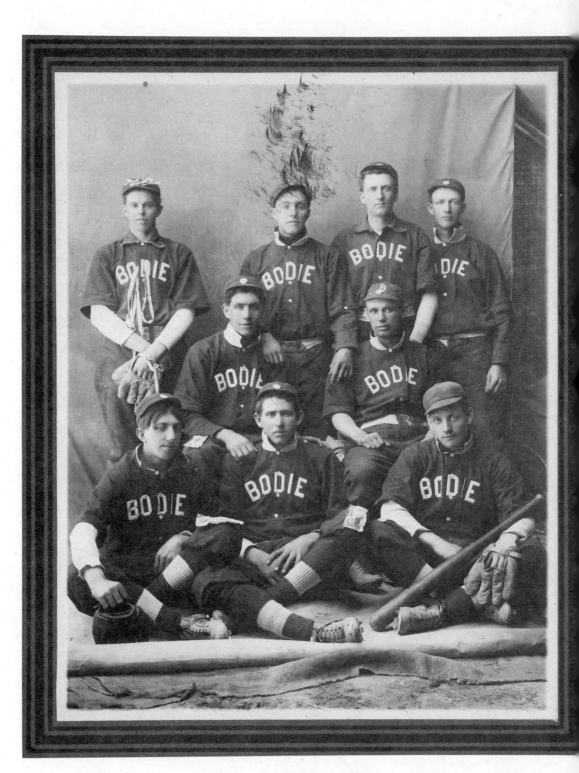

The Bodie Brass Band had been organized as early as 1878, as they were on hand at the opening that year of the Palace Club Rooms, an opulent saloon. A fixture in most Bodie celebrations, this band performed for many years in the 19th century.

As early as July 4, 1878 baseball was a popular recreation among the town's residents during the summer months. A home team, (opposite page) was later founded, and for many years it played against teams from other communities in eastern California and western Nevada.

Green St. in Winter

At an elevation of 8400 feet, Bodie's winters were always cold and windy, and usually brought heavy snowfalls. The winter of 1879 caught many unprepared, resulting in numerous deaths from exposure and pneumonia. Early in 1884 one storm dumped five feet of snow, followed by a second bringing three feet. Heavy snowfalls, coupled with high winds, generated drifts as high as rooftops, (left). With traffic at a standstill, skis and snowshoes were the only way to get from building to building.

Independence Day celebrations at Bodie were always festive. Horse-drawn conveyances paraded the main street in this 1909 scene. Residents of remote Bodie had to provide their own entertainment in other ways as well (below). The advent of the automobile gave rise to more frequent excursions and day outings. These well-dressed Bodieites are watching the horse races at the track at Booker Flat, prior to the construction of the track's grandstand.

By the late 1920's Bodie's slight population maintained only a few businesses on the main street (shown above looking north). Yet a fairly respectable tourist trade kept a few saloons open, even though Prohibition was still enforced. The Old Sawdust Corner Saloon, shown above just left of center and in the photograph below, occupied the strategic corner of Main and Green Streets. It was behind this building, which was last used as a morgue, that the fire of 1932 had its start.

Prospectors from other camps discovered the rich mines in the Bodie district, and in turn, adventurers from Bodie struck out eastward in search of gold and silver deposits. The businesses of Bodie became outfitting points for the prospectors, (top, opposite), who ventured east and south using not only teams of horses but mules as well. Three well-equipped prospecting parties prepare to strike out from Bodie, early in the 20th century.

Holiday scene on Bodie's Main Street, mid-1920's.

The fierce mining stampede of 1878 to these sage-covered hills resulted in much prospecting and the opening up of deep mines on Bodie Bluff and High Peak. By the late 1920's when this view of the wooden town of Bodie was taken, the Standard Co.'s mill still dominated the townsite. Earlier fires had reduced Bodie in size but in the great fire of 1932, many of the buildings shown here fell victim to flames.

Sometimes referred to as the Cain "Mansion," this tidy house was the home of James C. Cain, for decades Bodie's most prominent businessmen. First employed by a local lumber company, Cain later owned lumber barges on Mono Lake before he struck it rich on a 3-month lease on a portion of the Standard mine in 1880. Cain once leased the Bodie Railroad and lumber yard, owned the Bodie Stables, and in 1890 purchased the Bodie Bank. He even introduced the cyanide recovery process to Bodie, building the South End plant in the late 1890's. This house still survives.

Emil Billeb, last Super-intendent of the Mono Railway Co., and his wife Dolly, kept their Bodie house well-decorated with shrubbery. For many years around 1914 it was called "the only green spot in town."

THE GREAT FIRE OF 1932

Unlike most mining camps with a predominance of wood-frame buildings, Bodie did not experience a major fire during its peak boom years in the 1880's. However subsequent blazes did destroy much of the business district. The worst conflagration occurred on June 23, 1932, accidentally started by a young boy playing with matches in a wooden dwelling. Up in smoke went saloons, stores and many abandoned houses (top, opposite). In the lower picture the Standard Mill is visible at right beyond the smoke. By this time the mines were nearly silent and only a few hundred people lived in the district. Nevertheless the fire leveled many landmarks, leaving Bodie without most of the major buildings which played such an important part in its history.

"BODIE AFIRE" JUNE 23, 1932
BODIE, MONO COUNTY, CALIF.

"BODIE AFIRE" JUNE 23, 1932
BODIE, MONO COUNTY, CALIF.

THE BAD MAN OF BODIE

THE ENCOUNTER OF A "BLUFFER' WITH A MINING EXPERT— THE BULLY'S DISAPPOINTMENT

Washoe Pete was generally considered a "bluffer" by the critics of Bodie, and his wild exaggerations were the subject of merriment only in that "high old town." He was allowed to swagger and boast to his heart's content; and even when he drew his "nobby whistler" and shot the lights out of all the lamps in Ryan's saloon, the action only evoked a grin and the doubtful compliment that it was "purty fair shootin', and nigh as stiddy narve as Irish Tom showed when he popped away at that 'Bad Man' from Deadwood."

One day last summer Pete walked into Strobridge's saloon with the remark that he had "heerd the Last Chance was goin' to be sold, and they've sent up an expert to look into it."

The expert, a pale, small man, dressed in dusty gray, was standing at the bar, and looked around as the tall, would-be ruffian uttered these words.

"Thet's so, Pete," said one of the men present, "an' thet's the expert," pointing to the small man.

"You are an expert, eh!" shouted Pete, eyeing the man menacingly. "You're one of them fellows as allows he knows payin' mines, ar you?" Then, after a pause, during which he surveyed the stranger from head to foot, "Wall, you're the wust I ever saw. Experts is bad enough, but you're the slinkiest, meanest, wust coot to set yourself up to report on a mine I ever laid eyes on."

"I don't want to quarrel with you, sir," answered the expert.

"Ye'd better not, young feller; ye'd better not. I'm a whirlwind of the desert in a fight, and don't you forget it."

"I'm a man of peace; I carry no weapons, and, of course, I could not hope to stand before even a zephyr of the desert, let alone a wild, untamed whirlwind."

These deprecatory words only incensed the "bad man" still more, and, feeling that he had a "soft thing," proposed in his own mind to "play it for all it was worth," and gain a "record" by whipping his man.

"Look a heyer, stranger, I don't want no insinuations. Do I look like a zephyr? Say!" Here Washoe Pete shook his fist in the expert's face. "What d'ye mean by talkin' about zephyrs? I'm a tornado. I 'tear' when I turn loose. Zephyr (sneezing)! Why, I've a good mind to —"

"Please, mighty whirlwind, resistless tornado, don't hit me. You wouldn't strike a consumptive man, would you."

"Wouldn't I?" yelled the "fighter" in a terrible voice; "wouldn't I? I'd strike the side of a mountain!"

"But a sick man! pleaded the expert, "a man dying of consumption, an orphan, a stranger and a man of peace!"

"What're ye giving me? Do you know who I am?" fiercely demanded the whirlwind.

"You're a gentleman known in Bodie as Washoe Peter—at least I have heard you designated by that familiar appelation during my sojourn here," answered the expert, moving off.

"What else am I?" shrieked the rough, striding toward the cowering expert.

"A gentleman, I suppose. Honestly, I don't know your other name."

"Well, I'll tell you who I am;" and the tall man stood over the shrinking stranger as if about to topple upon him and annihilate him. "I'm bad; I'm chief in this yer camp, and I ken lick the man's says I ain't. I'm a ragin' lion of the plains, and every time I hit I kill. I've got an arm like a quartz stamp, an' crush when I go fur a man. I weigh a ton, an' earthquakes ain't nowhere when I drop."

"But I've only just been discharged from a hospital," replied the expert.

"I'll send ye back again!" and the stalwart "bluffer" caught the little man by the collar and hurled him upon the floor.

"It's unkind to use a poor, weak, suffering invalid that way," expostulated the expert, as he slowly arose from the floor. "Please don't joke so roughly. Let's take a drink and call it square. I'm very sorry that I have offended you."

"Ye think I'm joking, do ye—ye take me for a josh, eh? I'll show ye what I am afore I git through with ye. Ye don't play me for no tender-foot. I'm a native, I am, an' I've stood this yer foolin' long enough." Saying which he dashed the stranger against a table and drew a long knife.

As soon as the expert saw this he screwed his face into the most piteous shape, and throwing his hands up, cried: "I'm unarmed; I haven't got as much as a pen-knife on me. Please don't carve me; kick me to death if you must have my life, but for heaven's sake, don't stick that terrible thing into me."

Now, as Washoe Pete had no intention of using the knife—and thereby risking his neck—he was well pleased with the opportunity thus afforded him of using the deadly weapon, and after asserting his bloody intention, returning it to its sheath. He flourished the knife over the cringing expert three or four times, and then lowered it with the remark: "Why, dern your cowardly soul, I wouldn't disgrace the weepin' by shovin' it into ye. No, sir; but I'll plug ye," and he drew his revolver.

"I'm unarmed—I'm unarmed—don't ye hear me?" whined the expert.

"Go an' heel yourself then," retorted the bad man.

"I don't want to fight."

"I'll make ye fight. I"ll take ye at yer word, and kick ye to death."

"Please don't.

Washoe Pete laid his knife and pistol on the counter, and then strode rapidly to the spot where the expert was half crouching, half standing. By this time the saloon was full of men, all of them smiling at the picture before them, regarding it as the height of enjoyment—this lively encounter between the greatest braggadocio in the Sierra and a small, pale mining expert, new to the section and a stranger to the wild ways of the border ruffian.

"This thing has gone on 'bout long 'nough," yelled "bad man," stopping before the expert. "You've bin chinnin' to me till I'm riled. Squar' yourself—I'm goin' ter kick, an' a Comstock mule ain't a patchin' as a kicker to Washoe Pete—d'ye hear me?"

"One instant, please, Peter (I don't know your other name); are you sure you've got no other weapons about you? They might go off accidentally and injure some innocent party."

"That's all the weapins I've got, if the information'll ease yer sneakin' mind; and now I am goin' to begin kickin'. Clear the track. The woolly hoss has broken out o' the kerrell, and there'll be a Coroner's inquest in jest about seven minutes."

He raised his ponderous boot, but it did not swing. The little man straightened up like an unbent bow, and his left hand shot direct from his shoulder like the piston of a locomotive, striking Washoe Pete between the eyes and sending that worthy sprawling on the sawdust that covered the floor.

"I'm the Cyclone of the West," he shouted, as he bounded to the prostrate from of the "woolly hoss" and raised the braggart into a sitting position. The latter was dazed by the terrible blow he had received, and did not even throw up his guard when the expert drew back to strike again. Then the blows fell like thunderbolts upon the head and face of the "Whirlwind," inducing that individual to rise once more and attempt a defense. He made an effort to reach for his weapons, but the active expert flanked him and planted two terrible blows on his ears and neck.

The the "bad man" howled:

"Let up! I was only foolin'—can't ye take a joke, dern ye?"

"Ye think I'm jokin', do ye? Ye take me for a josh, eh? I'll show you what I am before I get through with ye. Ye don't play me for no tender-foot. I'm a native, I am; an' I've stood this yer foolin' long enough."

This apt reproduction of the native's speech a few moments previous, and its almost perfect similitude as regards tone, was too much for the good-natured crowd, and a roar of laughter greeted it that might have been heard beyond Bodie's bluff.

"I give in, dern ye, I give in! Can't ye take a man's word when he squeals?" shouted the "tornado," swinging his arms wildly, and staggering against the bar in his efforts to dodge the lightening stroke of the athletic expert.

"I'm a howling hurricane of wrath," shouted the expert, sending in both fists with terrific effect.

"Let up, won't you? I ain't a sandbag."

"Not much; you're only a 'ragin' lion o' the plains,'" and a swift left-hander lit upon the bully's nose.

"I give in," hoarsely ejaculated the expert's victim.

"Come on with your quartz stamps, old woolly hoss. When you hit you kill and you weigh a ton. Fetch in a couple of your earthquakes. Why don't you chaw my mane? You're a chief, are you? All right, chief, there's a neat one for you, and there's a couple more."

With these words the expert "countered" on the "bad man's" cheek, and then stretched him panting for breath on the floor with a "stinger" straight from the shoulder, inflicted upon the lower portion of the chest. Then the expert cooly called all hands to the bar to drink, and as the "bad man of Bodie" crawled away he was heard to mutter that he "didn't lay out to fall up against batterin' rams, no more'n he 'lowed he was game in front of a hull gymnasium."

THE NAMING OF BODIE

On about the 20th of November 1859, William S. Bodey and E. S. "Black" Taylor set out on foot from the little camp of Monoville to return to their small cabin near what is now the town of Bodie. The two men soon found themselves in the midst of a raging blizzard. Exhausted and unable to continue Bodey gave out, although they were less than two miles from their cabin. The younger Taylor attempted to carry him, but was too weak to make any headway in the snow. Finally he covered Bodey with their blankets before continuing alone.

So severe was the storm that he lost his way, and did not reach the cabin until 4 o'clock in the morning. Quickly Taylor built a fire, then changed into dry clothes. After cooking and eating a meal he felt warmed and strengthened enough to return for Bodey. Yet search as he might, Taylor could not find any trace of his partner in the deep snow drifts.

The following May, Taylor is reported to have found the body and buried it in a shallow grave. Another account states that a search party is reported to have found Bodey's body, taken it to Aurora, and interred it in the local cemetery under the auspices of the Free Masons. As Taylor was later killed by Indians, his story remained unverified.

By 1879, at the height of the boom, the fate of Bodey's body had been forgotten. When a badly-decomposed skeleton was found near where Bodey died, it was immediately believed to be his remains. Controversy quickly erupted. Even when Josiah Kirlew, a miner and prospector who had been in the region in 1860, related the account of Bodey's death and eventual burial in Aurora, he was ignored.

On Sunday, November 2, 1879 the citizens of Bodie held an elaborate funeral for the recently-discovered body which they felt was that of William Bodey. Following internment in the town's cemetery, a collection was taken for the purchase of an elaborate monument to grace the pioneer's grave. A sizeable amount was raised that day, prompting the order of a large granite spire cut from native stone.

So massive was the monument, and so busy was the stone-cutter during these violent years, that Bodey's memorial was not yet completed when President Garfield was assassinated in 1882. Raging with patriotic fervor, the town fathers told the stone-cutter to remove all traces of the prior inscriptions and replace them with others honoring the slain president.

Today Garfield's huge granite monument still stands in the Bodie graveyard, while the true fate of William Bodey remains uncertain.

Books about Bodie and the Nevada-California Border Country

NEVADA GHOST TOWNS & MINING CAMPS, by S. W. Paher. Large 8-1/2x11 format, 492 pages, 700 illustrations. About 668 ghost towns are described with directions on how to get to them. Every page brings new information and unpublished photos of the towns, the mines, the people and early Nevada life.

NEVADA TOWNS & TALES, by S. W. Paher, ed. 2 vols. 224 pp ea. 8-1/2x11. Chapters focus on Nevada's economic, social and geographical factors. Major sections discuss state emblems, gambling, politics, mining, business, ghost towns, prospecting, legends, early day women, ranching, native animals, industries, atomic testing, etc. Indexed. Color cover.

GOLDFIELD: BOOM TOWN OF NEVADA, by S.W. Paher. 16 pages, 9x12. Here is a summary of the boom days augmented by a careful selection of historic photographs showing the crowds, the businesses, and the ore.

NEVADA LOST MINES AND BURIED TREASURES, by Douglas McDonald, 128 pp., 6x9. Legends of lost mines in Nevada date from 1849 when west-bound emigrants discovered silver. The author recounts 74 of these tales of buried coins, bullion bars, stolen bank money, etc.

DEATH VALLEY GHOST TOWNS, VOL. I AND VOL. II, by S. W. Paher. 32 pp. each, 9x12, map. Though Death Valley's mineral history is best known for its colorful eras of borax mining, there were two distinct periods of gold and silver mining also. Panamint City, Calico, Rhyolite, Greenwater and others are listed.

COMSTOCK MINING AND MINERS, by Eliot Lord. 451 pp. This comprehensive history of the Comstock Lode traces the birth of the silver mining industry in America in turbulent Virginia City up to the date of original publication, 1883.

THE BIG BONANZA, by Dan De Quille. 488 pp. Subtitled, "An authentic account of the discovery, history and working of the Comstock Lode," this book covers all phases of the epic rise of Virginia City.

MINING DISTRICTS AND MINERAL RESOURCES OF NEVADA, by Francis C. Lincoln. 295 pp. This compilation gives a summary of each mining district in Nevada, all arranged by counties.

TONOPAH, NEVADA SILVER CAMP, by S.W. Paher. 16 pp., illus, map. The silver discovery at Tonopah in 1900 triggered the fast paced 20th century Nevada mining.

SKETCHES OF VIRGINIA CITY, N.T., by J. Ross Browne. 48 pp, illus. In 1860 the author commented extensively on the miners and their madness over minerals, the Chinese, the Indians, the stagecoach drivers, proprietors, barroom brawlers, etc. Charming, humorous cartoons of these appear in the book.

JULIA BULETTE AND THE RED LIGHT LADIES OF NEVADA, by Douglas McDonald. 32 pages, illus., map. Here is the best written historical sketch to date of Virginia City's famed prostitute who was murdered in 1867. An overview of Nevada prostitution occupies the last part of the book, augmented by interesting photographs.

MINING CAMP DAYS, by Emil W. Billib. 229 pp., illus. An observer-participant of early 20th century mining provides insights into the active days of Bodie, Tonopah and other Nevada and eastern California mining camps. Dozens of unpublished photographs augment a lively text.

For information and prices write to:
Nevada Publications
Box 15444 • Las Vegas, Nevada 89114